The Three Keys to Lasting Happiness and How to Obtain Them

by

Stephen Hawley Martin

WWW.OAKLEAPRESS.COM

The Three Keys to Lasting Happiness and How to Obtain Them © 2023 by Stephen Hawley Martin. All rights reserved. No part of this book may be used or reproduced in any manner whatsoever without written permission except in the case of brief quotations embodied in critical articles and reviews. For information visit:

www.oakleapress.com

Table of Contents

Chapter One: We All Want to Be Happy 5
    The Basis of Our Discontent
    Energy Is All There Is
    It's Time to Update Science
    Intelligence Came First
    Who and What Are You?

Chapter Two: Why You Exist 25
    Why Science Hasn't Caught Up
    The Essence of Campbell's Theory
    How Physical Reality Came About
    Karma Is How We Learn & Grow
    The Nature of Physical Reality
    The Ego and Soul Growth
    Thomas Campbell's Big TOE in Conclusion

Chapter Three: What's Really Going on 41
    Another Take on Reality & the Earth School
    The RA Material
    Brief Descriptions of the First Few Densities
    Things Go in Cycles
    Which Way Will Earth Go?

Chapter Four: Know Thyself 56

Chapter Five: Timeout to Determine Your Mission 66
    Take a Full Day to Pinpoint Your Path
    Obstacles Point to Your Path
    About Your Dharma

Chapter Six: Go for It 77

About Stephen Hawley Martin 83

"The first thing you have to know is yourself.
A man who knows himself can step outside
himself and watch his own reactions
like an observer."

— Adam Smith [1723-1776]

Chapter One
We All Want to Be Happy

The desire to be happy is universal among humans—don't you agree? Isn't that what all of us want? Isn't it why we go to Church, or alternatively, to a bar? Why we go on diets, workout at the gym, strive to make better grades, or do whatever we need to do in order to win that promotion?

So how do we go about achieving lasting happiness? As Ben Franklin reportedly said, "The constitution only guarantees the American people the right to pursue happiness. You have to catch it yourself."

You didn't learn in school how to catch it, which is why I've written this book. As far as I know, you won't find it anywhere else, except here. That's because the prevailing worldview in the western world today, and the advice given based on it, leads us away from happiness, not toward it. People are going to be unhappy or, at minimum discontented, as long as they believe the premise of western science as it is still taught in schools, which is that nothing exists except material substance. In a minute, I'll explain why, but first, if you took Psych 101, you know that Abraham Maslow believed that inherent in us are motivations that are unrelated to financial rewards. His five-stage model begins with basic physiological needs. Once we have reached the point of having enough to eat and a roof over our head, Maslow's hierarchy heads upward to include feeling secure, feeling confident, achieving self esteem and the respect of others, and finally to self-actualization. I suppose that's where Maslow would say you'll finally be happy. But is it? They may not admit it, but plenty of billionaires are unhappy, as are famous scientists and heads of governments.

What is self-actualization? It's likely different for different people. In this book, I'm going to show you how to identify your path to achieving respect, self-esteem, self-actualization, and ultimately something Maslow left out: lasting happiness. That's something that even the richest or most accomplished man or woman in the world may never achieve, so fasten your seatbelt and stick with me.

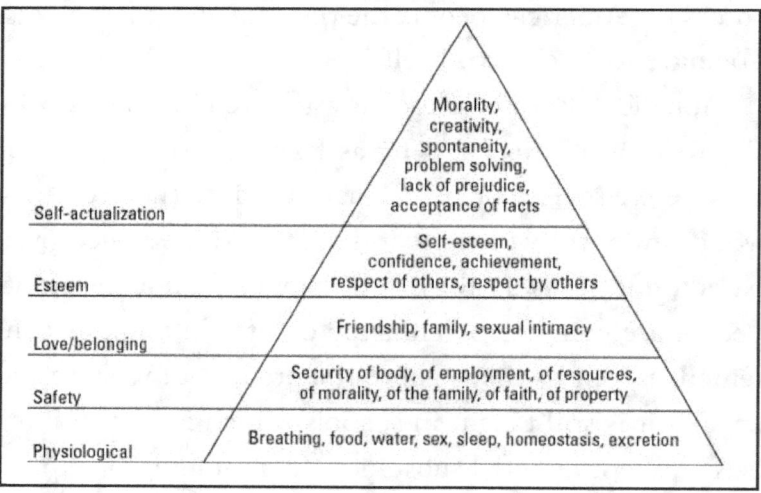

You see, I think it's safe to say the vast majority of people, at least in the United States, assume the way to fulfill growth needs and achieve happiness is to make something of ourselves, which in western society is to achieve wealth and power. But, according to a great deal of research that has been done over the last twenty or thirty years, attaining wealth and power might cause someone to be happy momentarily, but it will not bring happiness in the long run. Once you've made it to a certain level—accomplished the goal you set out to accomplish—you will get tired of that place, and soon you want to move up to an even higher plateau in search of an even greater feeling of accomplishment [or happiness] than what you experienced a short time ago. When you finally get there, that feeling of happiness will soon wear off, and you'll soon begin again like Finnegan. You might as well be a mouse on a treadmill—because you will never reach your destination, "happiness."

I recently watched a movie on Netflix that seems to point toward the most promising way to pursue happiness. It's a Shady Acres film called "Happy," a Wadi Rum Films production. "Happy" ponders contemporary happiness through visits with individuals around the globe who seem to have achieved it.

I'll give you a quick summary.

Depression, anxiety and other undesirable mental conditions have been studied for many years, but only recently have neuroscientists, psychologists and others begun seriously inquiring about the causes of happiness. The results so far indicate happiness increases the more a person is physically active, and the more he or she performs actions that benefit others rather than self—what in this book I'm going to call, "Service-to-Others." An important additional factor is how close an individual feels to his or her family and friends.

It turns out that obsessive pursuit of wealth, material goods, status, and image has the opposite effect. Without question, a difference exists in contentment between people who barely scrape by and those whose needs are comfortably met, but there is hardly any difference between those who are truly rich and those who feel they have what they need to get by. In other words, love isn't the only thing money can't buy. It can't buy happiness.

The film illustrates this through interviews with those who have found happiness in simple ways, or in togetherness. For example, the residents of a Danish co-housing community who share all domestic duties, including child rearing; a 60-year-old Brazilian surfer; Namibian tribes living off the land much as all mankind did millennia ago; a German ex-banker now working in one of Mother Teresa's charity wards; the cheerful populace of the island of Okinawa—world longevity capital due to healthy eating, valued traditions and constantly mingling generations. The film made the point that in contrast to Okinawa, mainland Japan has the globe's worst suicide rate. This was attributed to pervasive workaholic behavior, routinely leading to exhaustion and despair.

What it all comes down to is knowing and sensing that you are an integral part of the whole, and as one of the whole, you do your part by providing service to others. We all are born with talents and abilities. How we use them determines our happiness. There is, however, one more thing, and it has to do with knowing who you are—and I mean really knowing.

Here is what I will attempt in this book to convince you are the three keys to happiness:

1. The feeling and belief that you are an integral part of the whole.
2. Using your special talents and abilities in service to others.
3. The knowledge and belief that you are an eternal being.

The Basis of Our Discontent

For more than 160 years, the vast majority of scientists and science teachers—very likely unknowingly—have been propagating a belief that has been working against the achievement of happiness by anyone who believes what they've been taught. As of this writing, students in schools and colleges are still being told that nothing exists except matter. If this were true, which it most certainly is not, humans and other physical beings are nothing more than flesh, meat and bone robots with computer-like brains that create consciousness, which means that when they die, it's lights out—nothingness. Therefore, there can be no such thing as "eternal life." Nor can there be anything like an eternal soul that animates the body. It follows that those who believe this must come to the conclusion that life has no meaning beyond the experience of temporary pleasure from things like sex, good food and wine, and the accumulation of material wealth and power. Unfortunately, even if someone is good at accumulating, as stated above, doing so cannot keep that person happy or even satisfied for very long, and that's why those who think the material universe is all there is eventually come to the conclusion that "life's a bitch and then you die." The only logical course of action to avoid suicide is to grab all the gusto you can from life, even at the expense of others, such as Jeffery Epstein who prayed on teenage girls, and look what happened to him—suicide, likely arranged by one of his accomplices who didn't want his name to be exposed.

It totally escapes me how intelligent people can continue to believe Scientific Materialist nonsense. For even more reasons why materialism is baloney than those I am about to share with you, please read my book, *Life After Death, Powerful Evidence You Will Never Die*.

Energy Is All There Is

The truth is that "matter" doesn't actually exist as nineteenth century intellectuals thought of it when materialism made its debut. Quantum physicists have been saying this and demonstrating this for more than 100 years. Matter simply isn't real in the way Newtonian physics would have us believe, and in fact, Newtonian physics is not the way things actually are. Everything is energy, as in $E = MC^2$, i.e., "energy equals mass times the speed of light, squared."

Allow me to explain where I'm coming from so you can decide if I know what I'm writing about. I am the author of more than three-dozen books, including novels, business management books and a couple of dozen self-help and metaphysical titles. I've won about a half dozen national awards for my work, but here's what really qualifies me: I've had a near death experience (NDE) and a mind-blowing mystical experience. I've studied metaphysics, taken exams and attained the rank of Adept in the Rosicrucian Order—a community of mystics who study and practice the metaphysical laws governing the universe. And most important of all, over a three-year period I interviewed more than a hundred individuals who are researching the true nature of reality, including quantum physicists, near death survivors, remote viewing practitioners, scientists studying consciousness, NDEs, paranormal phenomena, psychic mediumship, and children's memories of past lives.

It's Time to Update Science

Let's take a look at the true nature of reality because the one you got from studying Scientific Materialism and Darwinian theory in school leads to a view of reality and humanity that is totally false, including the theory that evolution works solely by random mutations and survival of the fittest. Based on that theory, life came about purely by chance—I've heard various ways some think this happened such as lightning striking the right mixture of chemicals in the sea or a lagoon.

That made sense to people in the nineteenth century, but it cannot possibly be true based on what we know today. For life to come about required a DNA molecule to form since that is life's essential and basic building block. The question, then, is how could DNA have come about by accident or chance? A DNA molecule is the equivalent of a line of computer code that's six feet six inches (two meters) long composed of digits so small they are microscopic. It's analogous to a computer program that determines when and how to make proteins. Its double helix formation allows it to fold up so that it can be contained within the cell of a living organism. In other words, it is incredibly complicated.

Given that the earth is 4.5 billion years old and life appeared on Earth 3.77 billion years ago, there were only 730 million years for a DNA molecule to form, and it would have to have done so despite the Second Law of Thermodynamics, which is that the state of entropy of an isolated system will always increase over time. Even putting entropy aside—that left alone, things tend to fall apart rather than become more organized—a scientist who did the math would have to say that given that amount of time, the odds of something that complicated coming about by chance are about as close to zero as one can possibly get, and that's just the basic building block of life. Yet Scientific Materialists tell us that must have happened because of their belief—dare I say dogma—that only material substance exists. If true, consciousness and intelligence could not have come about until evolution produced a brain.

Intelligence Came First

A book published in 1975 refuted the idea that intelligence, consciousness, and awareness came about as a result of random mutations and survival of the fittest, i.e., Darwin's theory. In my opinion, it should have put an end not only to that theory but to Scientific Materialism in toto. Entitled *Intelligence Came First,* and it was compiled and edited by Ernest Lester Smith [1904-1992], a Fellow of the Royal Society—the prestigious scientific academy of the United Kingdom, dedicated to promoting excellence in science.

The book caused quite a bit of controversy back then. The premise is that, throughout the eons of evolution, needs have preceded the organs through which they are fulfilled—eyes, ears, taste buds, hearts, kidneys, and so forth. Since each new organ developed in response to a need, why would the brain be an exception? Smith and his colleagues put forth a compelling argument that intelligence came first, quite able to function in its own realm. This book has long been forgotten, perhaps by everyone except me, because Scientific Materialists shouted it down with a vengeance, but think of the intelligence that would be required to design any one of those organs. Could they all have come about by chance, i.e., random mutations followed by natural selection? Who in their right mind would argue that? Yet back in 1975, Scientific Materialists did just that with the result that Darwin's theory is still taught in schools and colleges as absolute truth.

Given the Second Law of Thermodynamics, the complexity of DNA, and the many complicated organs required for creatures to have evolved that now walk the land and swim in the waters of this planet, it seems virtually impossible that random mutations and survival of the fittest form the sole mechanism behind evolution. Darwin may have been on to something, however, in assuming survival of the fittest plays a role in the adaptation of creatures to changes in their environment, even though there's evidence that intelligence may guide that as well.

What follows is an example.

If you've ever been to the National Zoo in Washington, you've probably watched the giant pandas eating bamboo leaves. They take stalk after stalk and slide them between thumb and forefinger, stripping them, then popping this mouth-watering high-fiber food in their mouths. You may have wondered how these big guys got thumbs since primates are the ones with opposing digits. Pandas belong to the family Procyonidae (raccoons, kinkajous, etc.) of the order Carnivora, one of the hallmarks of which is that all five digits on the front paw point forward and have claws for ripping flesh.

On close inspection you'll find that the panda's thumb is not a thumb at all but a "complex structure formed by marked enlargement of a (wrist) bone and an extensive rearrangement of musculature." Not having the thumb needed to make bamboo eating easy, the panda took what he had to work with and evolved one of a makeshift variety. Could that really have happened by a series of random mutations? Of course not.

It is unfortunate that "Survival of the Fittest" is still taught as "settled science" in schools and colleges, not only because it isn't true, but because it lends support to the idea that some human races are more highly evolved than others. It was the underpinning of the imperialist belief in the nineteenth and twentieth centuries of "The White Man's Burden." On top of that, Scientific Materialists, who tend to be fervent supporters of Darwinian theory, would have us believe that, as mentioned above, humans are analogous to robots with computer-like brains, which naturally leads to the underlying assumption some models are better than others, just as many believe a Cadillac is superior to a Chevrolet. Such thinking led to Jim Crow laws passed in the American South and to the extermination of six million Jews by the Nazis in World War Two. Once science based on the false assumption that only matter exists is replaced with science that holds up to scrutiny, the belief that some races of humans are inherently inferior or superior to others will dissipate and eventually disappear because it is quite simply not true.

Who and What Are You?

Do not worry. I am not going to try in this book to convert you to any kind of religion. You don't have to belong to a religion, and you certainly do not have to believe in an anthropomorphic god to believe that you are a nonphysical, spiritual being having a temporary physical experience. I say this because I was an agnostic growing up, and today my concept of God is similar to what the Hindus call "Brahman," what some call, "The Source," what Jesus called "The Father," and what quantum physicists call "The Unified Field," and what I think of as a conscious force—the Life Force—that is the embodiment of "the urge to become."

The Three Keys

I became a Christian and was baptized sixteen years ago because, as a student metaphysics and a regular Churchgoer, I came to believe that Jesus was enlightened and knew what he was talking about—that he indeed shows us "The way, the truth, and the light." (John 14:6) I enjoy going to Church and belonging to a group of believers, even though we don't all believe exactly the same things. I actually went to Church and attended Bible studies for twenty years before officially becoming a Christian, which is how I know that one does not have to be a Christian per se to believe he or she is an eternal spiritual being. What follows, however, is evidence which I believe shows that, at the very least, Jesus was enlightened, and to my way of thinking, worthy of following. That doesn't mean you have to or should.

In Chapter Ten of the Gospel of John, Jesus explained that it wasn't he but the "Father," i.e., what Christians assume was God working through him that caused the miracles with which he was credited. As part of his explanation he said, "I and the Father are one." (See John 10:30 NIV.) This got him into hot water, and he was about to be stoned by irate Jews.

Jesus replied to the angry mob by saying, "I have shown you many good works from the Father. For which of these do you stone me?" (John 10:32 NIV)

The Jews answered, "We are not stoning you for any good work, but for blasphemy, because you, who are a man, declare yourself to be God." (John 10:33 NIV)

The Three Keys

Jesus then quoted Psalm 82:6: "Is it not written in your Law: 'I have said you are gods'?" (John 10:34 NIV)

By quoting this Scripture Jesus clearly was indicating that the Jews who wanted to stone him were "gods," as was he and every other human being—and that includes you—whether you are a Christian or a scientist, black, white, or brown.

By the way, I invite my fellow Christians who may scoff at this, as well as those who may think I am the one guilty of blasphemy, to consider these words also spoken by Jesus: "Whoever believes in me will do the works I have been doing, and they will do even greater things than these . . . " (See John 14:12 NIV) To believe in Jesus means, among other things, to believe what he said and taught is true, and that requires believing that we must have the ability, as he said in the Scripture just quoted, to perform miracles.

What I want to communicate is something mystics throughout history have understood: That All-Is-One, and your consciousness, my consciousness, and indeed everyone's consciousness is the single, unified, underlying "I AM" consciousness that Jesus called his "Father." It is what Christians call God and others refer to as Infinite Mind, The Divine Matrix, The Field, United Field, or Source that underlies, supports, informs—and indeed creates physical reality. You don't have to be religious to understand that—you just have to open your eyes and your mind. It is what Jesus understood, and that understanding and belief is what gave him the power to work miracles. When that has been taught in school for a couple of generations and everyone realizes it, racism will disappear, and the world will be a better place.

I can almost hear someone reading this thinking, "That's a lot of bull."

Really? You doubt that All-Is-One? If so, you ought to read Gary Zukav's book, *The Dancing Wu Li Masters*. In it, he explained quantum mechanics without using complicated mathematics. In summary, any quantum physicist will tell you that matter as envisioned by Newtonian physics does not actually exist. Everything is energy and everything is connected. Consider, for example, the following paragraph from that Gary Zukav's book:

> *. . . the philosophical implication of quantum mechanics is that all of the things in our universe (including us) that appear to exist independently are actually parts of one all-encompassing organic pattern, and that no parts of that pattern are ever really separate from it or from each other.*

Alan Watts [1915-1973], a twentieth century philosopher and interpreter of Zen Buddhism, answered children's questions concerning why they were here, where the universe came from, where people go when they die and so forth with a parable about God playing hide and seek. Watts told them God enjoys the game, but has no one outside himself to play with since he is All-that-Is. He overcomes this problem of not having any playmates by pretending he is not himself. Instead he pretends that he is me and you and all the other people and the animals and rocks and stars and planets and plants and in doing so has wonderful and wondrous adventures. These adventures are like dreams because when he awakes, they disappear. Watts wrote:

> *Now when God plays hide and pretends that he is you and I, he does it so well that it takes him a long time to remember where and how he hid himself. But that's the whole fun of it—just what he wanted to do. He doesn't want to find himself too quickly, for that would spoil the game. That is why it is so difficult for you and me to find out that we are God in disguise, pretending not to be himself. But when the game has gone on long enough, all of us will wake up, stop pretending, and remember that we are all one single Self—the God who is all that there is and who lives forever and ever.*

It will no doubt be shocking to some to think of themselves as God, but Watts was talking about the core essence that is beyond the ego and deeper within than the personal unconscious, the collective unconscious, the archetypes and so on. As Joseph Campbell [1904-1987] said in the PBS TV series, *The Power of Myth,* "You see, there are two ways of thinking 'I am God.' If you think, 'I, here in my physical presence and in my temporal character, am God,' then you are mad and have short-circuited the experience. You are God, not in your ego, but in your deepest being, where you are at one with the non dual transcendent."

Joseph Campbell also said, "God is within you! You yourself are the creator. If you find that place within you from

The Three Keys

which you brought this thing about, you will be able to live with it and affirm it, perhaps even enjoy it, as your life."

As indicated by the above text, that we are all One Life that arises from the "non dual transcendent" is not something I came up with. It is something mystics and enlightened beings have known for thousands of years. But if you believe what you were taught in school or college by your science teachers that nothing exists except matter and that life and evolution happened by accident, you believe as mentioned above that the body can be compared to a machine and the brain to a computer. On the other hand, if you are a Christian, you likely believe you were created by God and that when your body dies your spirit will go to heaven, which is what will actually happen.

No matter what you now believe, I urge you to stick with me, and please keep an open mind as you read ahead. I'm going to relate a theory that I developed after more than forty years of research and study, and I will cite facts to back it up. Not only does it explain what caused the Big Bang and how life on earth came to be, it makes clear that faith is not required to believe we are all one and your consciousness will continue after your body dies. It also indicates that you possess what likely has been until now undreamed of power and that we are spiritual beings having a physical experience. There is no room for racism in any of that.

Two mysteries have captivated the human imagination for thousands of years. The first is why the universe exists at all. Why is there something rather than nothing? The

The Three Keys

second is that conscious minds exist to perceive it. An ancient idea is that the mystery of consciousness and the mystery of existence are intimately connected, and perhaps surprisingly, there are now a growing number of philosophers and scientists who take this possibility seriously.

Beginning in the first half of the twentieth century, cosmologists began learning a great deal about the early universe by analyzing cosmic background radiation and other phenomena. Using powerful telescopes they were able to see that there are many galaxies, and due to their shift toward the red end of the spectrum of light, that those farthest away are moving away from us faster than those in closer proximity. As a result, cosmologists are able to peer deeply into the past and infer the state of the universe in what is thought to be its first fractions of a second. But where did it all come from? What existed before the Big Bang?

Physicists have proposed that the spark of existence had its origin in a quantum fluctuation, triggering an explosive chain reaction, leading to the still evolving universe we inhabit today. This narrative, however, presupposes the laws of quantum mechanics. As British Biochemist Rupert Sheldrake said in a TED Talk, "[Scientists today say] give us one free miracle and we'll explain the rest.' And the one free miracle is the appearance of all the matter and energy of the universe, and all the laws that govern it, from nothing in a single instant." Suffice it to say that rather than explaining existence, current scientific theories of the origins of the universe have simply pushed things back to a point that raises the question, "What existed before the Big Bang?" Could it all have come from nothing? Although that is apparently what some scientists believe, it doesn't make sense. As the song in *The Sound of Music* goes, "Nothing comes from nothing, nothing ever could."

Instead of beginning with nothing, it seems logical that the challenge of explaining existence should focus instead on defining a self-existing ground of being for which no explanation is required. Physicists have proposed that the true ground floor of reality is the seething quantum realm of particles, forming in and out of existence. While this level of reality surely exists, there is no clear reason why the primordial situation should be constrained by quantum physics. A deeper level of explanation seems to be required, and one possibility is that consciousness is the ground of being. How seething quantum particles or "strings" came to be the ground of reality calls out for an explanation, but in theory, consciousness can explain itself. A unique feature of consciousness is that it does not appear grounded in anything beyond itself. The conscious self is self-producing insofar that it exists only in and to itself. As René Descartes [1596-1650] famously said, "I think therefore I am."

Moreover, without consciousness, it would not matter if anything existed because no sentient being would perceive it. I am reminded of a question that my philosophy professor once asked on a test, "If a tree falls in the woods and no one and no thing were there to hear it, would it make a sound?" The answer is "No, for there to be a sound, someone or something has to hear it." You can say the same about physical reality. Would physical reality exist if no one and no thing were here to perceive it? The same logic says, "No, observation is what creates physical reality."

I intuit someone reading this saying to him or herself, "Yeah, but the brain creates consciousness."

Not so. As I have written about extensively in other books, the conclusion drawn after sixty years of research by the Division of Perceptual Studies [DOPS] at the University of Virginia School of Medicine is that the brain does not create consciousness. The brain is a receiver of consciousness like a cell phone—a receiver that integrates consciousness with the body.

My theory—and a similar theory you will read about in the next chapter—is based on the idea that consciousness just is. Your personal consciousness seems to belong to you because you have memories stored in your unconscious mind. You also have a name and perhaps a job and a history that was created while inhabiting your current physical body, and all that gives you a sense of identity. When your consciousness leaves your body, you will continue to have those memories—if not indefinitely, at least for a while based on extensive research by DOPS into reincarnation and near death experiences. Even if those memories dissipate and your consciousness eventually dissolves into your higher self and ultimately into the universal consciousness, that universal consciousness will still be you. I say this because consciousness is the "I AM," the Silent Observer at the back of your mind. As Alan Watts said a few paragraphs ago, "When the game has gone on long enough, all of us will wake up, stop pretending, and remember that we are all one single Self—the God who is all that there is and who lives for ever and ever."

So, there you are. You are an integral part of the whole—you are at one will every other human being and indeed all-that-is. You are an eternal spiritual being having a temporary physical experience and you will exist for eternity. Once you accept that and believe it, you will possess numbers One and Three of the Three Keys to lasting happiness.

The question is, why? Why does physical reality exist? As we will see in the next chapter, it exists for three reasons. This is important to know about in order to obtain and embrace the other key.

Chapter Two
Why You Exist

I'm going to relate a theory developed and put forth by an astrophysicist in an attempt to explain why we are here on Earth, which I think comes very close to the truth—although perhaps in a metaphorical way. Thomas Campbell is the astrophysicist's name, and he goes into great detail about his theory in a book called, *My Big TOE*. "TOE," by the way, stands for "Theory of Everything."

Albert Einstein once said, "The aim of all science is to cover the greatest number of empirical facts by logical deduction from the smallest number of hypotheses or axioms."

Campbell's theory is based on two:

1. What he calls "The Fundamental Process" of evolution, and
2. There is a single source of all that is, and it is primordial consciousness.

Concerning The Fundamental Process, Campbell maintains that all things and all systems are actively in the process of change, whether they are animal, vegetable, mineral, technological, or organizational. Inanimate physical objects seek the minimum, i.e., lowest possible, energy states. Animate physical objects (live organisms) seek procreative potential and survival. That seeking action is "The

Fundamental Process." As an aside, I call it "the urge to become," which in other books I have labeled "The Secret of Life."

Campbell says the evolutionary purpose of consciousness is to seek states of lower entropy, and therefore, the Fundamental Process dictates that all life should evolve toward greater profitability. Profitability is defined by the degree of immediate success an entity has in dealing with the evolutionary pressures created by its environment. The Process involves each entity moving into all the possibilities open to it. The winners survive. This happens not so much by deliberately making choices as it does by trying everything possible, although Campbell does believe that at times change is in reaction to the environment, i.e., that organisms often are able to adapt. However it may occur, evolution moves toward more complex, capable, and highly organized, what he labels "lower entropy" forms, by building upon or enhancing the earlier, simpler forms.

This is an important aspect of his theory—that the evolutionary pressure of self-improvement moves consciousness toward higher quality and lower entropy states. This is the equivalent to moving consciousness to brighter, more aware, and more highly organized configurations. Lower entropy produces higher quality, which means that the consciousness system has more energy available to do work (to more profitably organize).

"Love" is the word Campbell uses to describe how a low entropy, high quality consciousness interacts with other beings. Love is the result of evolution and an essential element in evolution's scheme. A mother bird, fox, or rabbit that does not love her offspring might neglect to feed them and thereby let them die. It follows that highly sentient beings like ourselves who are predisposed to love and support the wellbeing of others will likely form synergistic groups, nations, and a world whose residents will have a higher probability of survival than those who are not so inclined.

The capacity, ability and willingness of an individual to love are indications of how much entropy his or her consciousness contains. In other words, love capacity is a direct measure of entropy within consciousness. It seems to me this hints at the world's coming transition to "Fourth Density," which is something we will discuss in the chapter after this one.

Why Science Hasn't Caught Up

Thomas Campbell makes clear why he believes no scientist, not even Albert Einstein, has been able to come up with a viable "Theory of Everything" [TOE] that explains intuition, mind, consciousness, the paranormal, and the so-called "spooky" and "participating observer" phenomena of quantum physics. Current science cannot even explain how physical reality came to be, except to say it happened with a big bang. The reason is simple. As previously discussed, the fundamental tenet of science today is that nothing exists other than physical reality. Yet anyone paying attention knows a tremendous amount of evidence to the contrary has come to light in recent years. Like everyone except the little boy watching the parade in which the king wore no clothes, I suspect many contemporary scientists can see the truth but are reticent to say so for fear of being ostracized.

Let me say as an aside that when I was researching a book I wrote called *A Witch in the Family* about my ancestor, Susannah North Martin, who was hanged as a witch in Salem, Massachusetts in 1692, I learned where the idea originated that matter is all that is. Ironically, it did not come from a scientist. It came from an English philosopher named Thomas Hobbes (1588-1679) who was railing against the belief in witchcraft and in magic that was widespread in his day. Hobbes wrote that, other than God who created it, matter is all that is, and therefore ghosts, goblins, and such are figments of the imagination. Although he offered no proof or rationale for this assertion, it was soon latched onto as a basic scientific tenet—a dogmatic belief—and it became an important factor leading to the Age of Enlightenment and the growth of modern science.

Let me interject here that without doubt the Age of Enlightenment and modern science were and are good things, of course, and have made life immensely better for humanity, even though they came about as results of an erroneous assertion. Nowadays, however, having pushed everything back to the dawn of material reality—the Big Bang—the time has come to let go of that particular seventeenth-century notion.

As Thomas Campbell writes, "Requiring the big picture reality to be described exclusively in terms of the little picture reality is an incredibly dumb idea. It is an amusing fact that many of the world's scientists are totally stumped by this trivial concept. If you cannot physically define and control consciousness and side effects, then neither can be verified to exist as an independent entity or real phenomenon. Consciousness is seen as a hallucination of a physical, biological process while side effects are seen as hallucinations of psychological processes. By believing that what is real is delusional and what is delusional is real, scientists have boxed themselves into a small corner of reality that does not contain the answers they are looking for."

The Essence of Campbell's Theory

According to Thomas Campbell, everything evolved from primordial consciousness, which he calls "Absolute Unbounded Oneness," or [AUO]. He likens AUO to an energy form that, like earth's early carbon-based bio-forms, has the potential to evolve. In other words, AUO represents the primordial substance of consciousness, not the attribute of being conscious.

What Campbell calls AUM [Absolute Unbounded Manifold], is dim consciousness or AUO that has evolved into brilliant consciousness. I prefer to call AUM "Infinite Mind." Others no doubt would prefer the term, "God." Sometimes it's called "The Source," "The Field," "The Unified Field," or "The Divine Matrix." As mentioned earlier, Jesus called it "The Father." The Hindu word for non-dual pure consciousness is "Brahman." It seems to me all those terms are pointing to the same thing. Going forward, I'll call it "Infinite Mind" or "The Source" just to keep it simple.

The Three Keys

Infinite Mind's most basic function and purpose is to implement the Fundamental Process. In other words, it is to evolve, grow, and to become more profitable by expanding into all available possibilities and maximizing the return on its evolutionary investments by supporting the winners. In order to do so, Infinite Mind began by producing at least two and probably many many more concentrations of consciousness so that they could interact. That way, it isolated a few pieces of itself and granted them unique boundaries so each could be separately distinguishable and self-contained—in other words, you and me and what I think of as every other separate little whirlpool of ground-of-being consciousness that you can see in the flesh filling football stadiums every fall and on blankets on beaches in summer. The objective was for them to interact and thereby learn and expand the boundaries of their consciousness as well as the consciousness of the whole—what I call Infinite Mind.

Campbell used the following metaphor in a YouTube video to help people form a mental image of how this might have taken place: Consider that AUM (Infinite Mind) is a bed sheet, and that a couple of children make puppets in the sheet by forming it around their hands and placing rubber bands around their wrists to keep the bubbles in the sheet in place around their hands. It's still all one sheet, but the children now have puppets they can use to interact with one another.

As alluded to above, those puppets are you and me and all other sentient beings, which means, of course, that we are all connected with each other and everything else because at the fundamental level we all share the same consciousness or mind. This explains the "spooky action at a distance" phenomenon—that objects separated by great distance can instantaneously affect each other's behavior—they are part of the same mind, and when it comes to mind, there is no such thing as distance. It also explains the "participating observer" phenomenon in quantum mechanics research such as the double-slit experiment that I describe in detail in a couple of my books. What the observer knows or doesn't know determines the outcome of the experiment because the observer and the components of the experiment are facets of the single mind that forms reality.

According to Campbell, we are and remain fully integrated pieces of the larger system with access to the capabilities and capacities of that system. Our individual potential is the potential of the entire Infinite Mind. To what extent we actualize or achieve that potential through self-optimization or self-improvement is up to us. Individuated units of consciousness, once created, persist within AUM-Infinite Mind indefinitely and have the opportunity to evolve to the limits of AUM's capacity, each by developing and following its own personal path.

It boils down to this: if we evolve the quality of our being sufficiently, we will return to the Source and actually become the Source. Because we contain the potential of the whole, we will not be swallowed up by the consciousness system, but rather we will become a fully integrated and a fully aware part of it.

Campbell maintains that AUM (Infinite Mind), and all manifest reality, is digital. Like computer software, it is composed of X's and O's, Ones and Twos, Yes and No, or Ying and Yang. One of the attributes of digital systems is that as long as memory is never purged, no information is ever lost. In other words, your individual self will be maintained even once you become merged with the whole, and you will retain your individual awareness—your sense of "I Am." As digital consciousness beings we are truly immortal unless the bits that represent us become distorted beyond repair, irredeemably negative, or are deleted from memory. It appears then, that unless you are Adolf Hitler, Jeffrey Dahmer, or Jeffrey Epstein you are likely to be around forever, and who knows, maybe they will be, too.

How Physical Reality Came About

According to Campbell, in the nonphysical realm, a mind can change, grow, and evolve more rapidly than in a physical body because it contains more degrees of freedom and fewer constraints. As a result, steady growth and development of consciousness occurred in the beginning until growth to higher and still higher qualities of consciousness diminished to an unacceptably slow rate. This phenomenon of slowing down happens nowadays, and it happened before physical reality was created. Think about it. At points in time—say at two years, and at 19, and again maybe at 40—individuated consciousness units (you and me) tend to begin thinking we know it all, and that we have learned all we need to know. In other words, we tend to fall into dead-end belief traps like scientists who continue to believe physical reality is all there is. According to Campbell, that is what happened to individuated units of consciousness before the Big Bang took place some 12 to 14 billion years ago.

To counter this stagnated growth issue, a way was devised for units of consciousness to retain the lowered entropy and underlying wisdom they had achieved, but to periodically start over without the baggage of accumulated erroneous beliefs and misinformation that inhibited further growth. This is the rationale behind the existence of nonphysical individuated units of consciousness (souls) and separate physical vehicles for those units—bodies. I'm talking about reincarnation, of course.

If you are interested or don't believe reincarnation is possible, I have gone into detail about research into reincarnation in other books. Research on this subject began at the University of Virginia in 1962. In 1967 a unit of the UVa medical school [DOPS] was formed to study reincarnation and other topics involving consciousness such as near death experiences. I have twice interviewed the head of DOPS, Jim B. Tucker, M.D., who is also a child psychologist. Based on more than 2600 cases of children's memories of past lives that have been studied by UVa researchers, there can no longer be any doubt that reincarnation does in fact occur. If you want to delve into the subject, I suggest you read my book *REINCARNATION: Good News for Open-Minded Christians and Other Truth-Seekers.*

The reason reincarnation is no longer part of Christian canon is that the Emperor Justinian [527-565] overrode the pope and forcibly had it removed at the Second Council of Constantinople in 553 AD. An author who wrote a book on this topic—who happens to have been a retired Baptist pastor—told me in an interview that he believes Justinian's motivation was that of exerting and maintaining control over his subjects. If people thought they would have additional chances to get to heaven, they might not fall in line and obey church rules. Fear, as everyone knows, is a great motivator.

So where does all this shake out? The bottom line according to Thomas Campbell is that the phenomenon of birth, death and rebirth was the impetus for creating physical reality, which occurred in a Big Bang, the evidence of which can still be detected today. The result is that we inhabitants of this reality have the benefit of being able to start over every so often with a relatively clean slate. The benefit from the point of view of the Infinite Mind is that learning takes place faster than it otherwise would. Being able to make a new start without the erroneous beliefs of a previous life but with the underlying wisdom that was gained enables us to increase the quality of our consciousness while continuing to exercise free will.

Our souls, or higher selves if you prefer that term, exist at all times in the nonphysical realm. Non-physical reality apparently is not terribly different from the physical reality in which we are apparently tricked into believing is our home. There are bosses, judges, good guys and bad guys, conflict, and competition there as well. Many of "individuated units of consciousness" (Campbell's term for human or human-like beings) of the nonphysical dimension are what were known as "gods" to the ancient Greeks, Romans, Egyptians, Mayans, and so forth. There are also entities that help and guide those of us currently in physical form—what some call "Guardian Angels," and others call, "Guides."

When our bodies die, the soul assimilates whatever learning it can from the just concluded lifetime. According to Campbell, leaving behind a lifetime and passing from the physical to the nonphysical can be compared to waking from a dream. While a person may remember the dream for a while, eventually the memory fades. I happen to know, however, this is not always the case. Research conducted by UVa to do with children's memories of past lives indicates some do remember their most recent previous lifetime, and research by regression therapists indicates that under hypnotism, some people can remember lives that took place thousands of years ago. I can recall bits and snippets of lives that took place in the twentieth century, the nineteenth century, the seventeenth century, one in what I think is the twelfth century, and another about seven hundred and fifty years BC.

Karma Is How We Learn & Grow

The concept of karma as revealed by the twentieth century's most documented psychic, Edgar Cayce (1877-1945), makes sense in Campbell's representation of reincarnation. According to Edgar Cayce's psychic readings, karma is not punishment, but rather, it is a learning tool.

An entity (human soul) will continue to meet similar, difficult situations to those that created the karma until the entity begins making better choices. It is as though we entities are like the character in the movie *Groundhog Day* who is forced to experience the same day over and over until he reacts to each situation with love instead of cynicism. Only then does he handle things correctly. Once the quality of his consciousness has evolved to a level that produces right action, he not only gets the girl, he is finally able to move on to February 3.

Does an entity continue to evolve in the nonphysical realm once a life is over? The answer is yes and no. He or she will continue to evolve but not necessarily in the nonphysical realm. Unless an entity has reached a level at which it is no longer beneficial to do so, he or she will return to the physical.

The Nature of Physical Reality

According to Thomas Campbell, physical existence is a virtual interactive experience designed to facilitate the evolution of consciousness. He says we humans and other sentient beings, both physical and nonphysical, can be compared to simulated entities in a virtual reality game created by a computer, i.e., avatars. A big difference is that they exist in a computer, and we exist in the mind of the evolving AUM/Infinite Mind, but even so, computer-game entities are operationally quite similar. Other differences have mostly to do with the quality and richness of the input data from our primary five sensors. Campbell points to the extensive use of parallel processing, feedback loops, and the capacity of our dedicated processing equipment (our brain and central nervous system) to indicate the semblance to our own digital creations, although he does note that we humans are radically different when it comes to motivations, limitations, substance, and construction. The single most significant difference is our free will to make choices that reflect and define the quality of our evolving consciousness. We are superior in that we possess a nonphysical component and a will that is free to make decisions that express intent and complex motivations. In other words, we have emotions, and we have a soul or higher self, which computer avatars do not.

According to Campbell, our physical universe is just one of a very large number of both physical and nonphysical realities. Read his book if you want to know more in that regard.

The Ego and Soul Growth

Our egos often slow down or block our soul growth, and they can even cause an entity to become narcissistic and evil. To understand how this can happen, we must first understand fear. At the deepest level, fear is generated by ignorance that exists within a consciousness of low quality. Therefore, the lower someone's consciousness and the greater their ignorance, the more likely they are to become evil. Fear and high entropy are mutually supportive in that one creates and encourages the other. Needs, wants, expectations, and desires are generated by the ego as part of its shortsighted strategy to reduce the anxiety produced by fear. Desire is generated by wants and needs, although not all desire is fear-based or counterproductive. Basic lower-need desires such as sex and hunger are not necessarily fear-based, and the desire to improve oneself if the motivation is correct can be a strong, positive incentive. In general, however, when Campbell speaks of desire he is speaking of desire that arises in response to ego demands.

An individual's ego and intellect work together to produce and justify those wants, needs, and desires that are required to prevent fear from adversely affecting the functional, operative awareness of the individual. Ego's mission is to make sure the individual always feels good about him or herself. No ploy or deceit is off limits as long as it can be justified.

Spirituality, as Campbell refers to it, is equivalent to consciousness quality. One becomes more spiritual—demonstrates a higher consciousness quality and makes progress on a spiritual growth path—by lowering the entropy of his or her consciousness. A consciousness of lower entropy produces a consciousness of higher quality. In other words, the level of spirituality and the degree of consciousness quality is inversely related to the entropy the individuated consciousness contains.

A person's spiritual quality is directly related to a person's capacity to love. By lowering the entropy of our individual consciousness, we also lower the entropy of the entire consciousness system. As alluded to earlier, that is what our existence is about and what AUM/Infinite Mind is in the process of doing. This is not to say, however, that some entities do not use their free will to evolve at least for a while toward the opposite of love. Some obviously attempt to control the environment through power and intimidation. A quick look at this morning's headlines will likely reveal how rampant and pervasive that is in this reality. This will be addressed in the next chapter. In the next chapter, an entity oriented this way will be described as following the "Service-to-Self" path.

Thomas Campbell's Big TOE in Conclusion

Each of us, and all of us are on the path of evolution whether or not we realize it. AUM/Infinite Mind has set everything up for us to succeed. It has provided a physical-reality learning lab with interactive feedback (karma). In addition, nonphysical beings are assigned to help us in every way allowed under the rules that AUM/Infinite Mind has established. These beings are focused directly on individuals—you and me included—to plan, encourage and guide our spiritual growth, i.e., the growth in quality of our consciousness. Moreover, some of us, such as Buddha and Jesus who have outgrown this dimension return to physical reality as teachers to help point the way. Nevertheless, we humans often manage to dilute, divert, and distort their helpful instruction by burying the essential truth of their message under a blanket of dogma. It seems to me this is certainly true with respect to some churches.

The book Campbell wrote explaining his theory is 824 pages long. It should go without saying that my summary is the nutshell version. If what I have presented has whetted your appetite for more details, there are plenty in Thomas' book, and so I suggest you read a copy. But wait to do so until after you've finished reading this book. You started it because you'd like to achieve lasting happiness, and so you need to finish it so that you will know what you need to know to catch it.

My summary of Campbell's Big TOE was meant to help you put your mind around the fact that you are an integral part of the whole, a spark of the Source or Infinite Mind, which is one of the three keys to lasting happiness. In the next chapter we're going to look at the possibility that a big change might be coming to Earth—that there's a battle going on and your actions can help determine the winner. It will also help you understand and see that using your special talents and abilities in service to others is indeed one of three keys to lasting happiness.

Chapter Three
What's Really Going on

Before it incarnates, each soul enters into a sacred contract with the Universe to accomplish certain things. It enters into this commitment in the fullness of its being. Whatever the task that your soul has agreed to, all of the experiences of your life serve to awaken within you the memory of that contract, and to prepare you to fulfill it.

— Gary Zukav,
Bestselling Author of
The Seat of the Soul (1989)

Did we incarnate and enter the physical realm with a specific mission or missions to accomplish as stated by Gary Zukav in the quotation above? Many believe so. Most certainly this is true if our task in life is to evolve our consciousness, or if it is to help others do so.

I believe my primary mission in this life is one this book and others I've written is intended to accomplish, which is to explode the myth that matter is all there is and to spread the word that we are eternal spiritual beings having a temporary physical experience. The world will be a much better place when the majority of us recognize these facts and become aware that the evolution of consciousness is what the University of Earth exists to bring about.

Like most humans alive today, another mission of mine is to overcome and jettison karma, and in doing so, to enable my consciousness to evolve. This brings to mind a book that as editor and publisher of The Oaklea Press I recently brought to market called, *What My Life's Been All About: And Why You're Here on Earth.* It's by James King, whom I've come to call Jim, a British gentleman who lives in southern France. Closing in on age 90, he decided to catalog key events in his life that led him where he is today—mentally, spiritually, and physically.

Jim came into this world this time on the Third of July 1933, and he arrived with a lot of psychological baggage to unload. Fortunately, but more likely by choice, he was born to a family that passed along to him abilities that served him well. They were his mother's musical talent, father's intellectual prowess, his grandfather's talent for generating energy healing (Reiki), and his grandmother's psychic capability. Jim inherited these attributes, which in time enabled him to see through the falsehood perpetuated by western culture that matter is all there is and to accomplish his mission—which was to overcome and unload the huge amount of psychological baggage he had accumulated during several previous lifetimes.

Having become friends, Jim sent me what he had written. While reading it, I was reminded of the Nineteenth Century German philosopher Arthur Schopenhauer [1788–1860], who observed in one of his essays that when an individual reaches an advanced age and looks back over his or her lifetime, the lifetime will seem to have followed a consistent plan as though composed by a master storyteller or novelist. Specific events and the meeting of individuals that seemed at the time to have come about by chance turn out to have been essential components in a constant storyline.

This brings up a question:

> "Why do you suppose you were born when and where you were and to your particular parents?"

Chances are you have lived many times. Does something that happened in a past life need to be addressed in this one? For me, it was unfinished business from a life in China as a holy man approximately 2,800 years ago, during which my mission of passing along esoteric knowledge to others was thwarted.

I believe everyone alive today came to earth with a mission to accomplish, but only a small percentage will actually accomplish his or hers in this lifetime. This is truly a shame because it doesn't have to be. By knowing the truth and spreading the truth to others, you can help turn around this situation.

Another Take on Reality & the Earth School

So that you will have additional knowledge that might enable you to help me spread the truth as well as for you to achieve lasting happiness, in the rest of this chapter we are going to take a look at a concept of reality more and more seekers are coming to accept as true.

Back in the 1980s, a few years after beginning my quest to understand the true nature of reality, I read a book entitled, *The RA Contact: Teaching the Law of One,* by Don Elkins, Carla L. Rueckert, and James Allen McCarty. A fellow seeker had recommended it to me as a "must-read." He was so enthusiastic about the material that I forced myself to read most of it, but frankly, at that time my fellow seeker was way ahead of me in his understanding of what life is all about. I felt the book was much too far out and too far fetched to be true, and so I dismissed it.

I now realize we often react to anything that does not resonate with us with a knee-jerk dismissal because we don't know what we don't know. The truth is, I knew too little at that time to objectively consider RA and The Law of One. I simply wasn't ready for it. A couple of years ago, however, I was reintroduced to the RA material. Having come a long, long way on my journey of understanding, this time I was amazed at what RA had to say. It was as though all the disparate facts that I now understood about reality were brought together and crystallized into a view that made perfect sense. In other words, what RA had to say made everything I'd learned fall into place. Moreover, it seemed preordained that this would happen now in what appears to be a watershed moment. That's why I am not only going to tell you what RA reveals that will greatly benefit you, I am also going to tell you why I think it makes perfect sense and has a high probability of being true.

The RA Material

There are five books in The Law of One series, the material for which was channeled in the early 1980s by the three individuals listed above as authors of the work. I will refer to RA with the pronoun "they" because RA claims to be a "group soul" of an advanced civilization that evolved on the planet Venus while earth was still primarily a smoldering rock. I'm sure many readers are going to think that is completely nuts, but according to NASA, Venus once was hospitable to life. Based on computer modeling done in 2016 of the planet's ancient climate by scientists at NASA's Goddard Institute, Venus is thought to have had a shallow liquid-water ocean and habitable surface temperatures for up to two billion years of its early existence. For reasons I will not go into because they are outside the scope of this book, according to RA, life evolved and advanced on Venus to a higher form than now exists on Earth, what they call "Fourth Density." In other words, the souls that now form RA evolved much faster than we have been evolving here, they have continued evolving, and they have now achieved Six Density. The group soul called RA says they now exist in a non-physical dimension of reality and that they are composed of approximately six million like-minded souls all of whom evolved on Venus. Even though they have combined into a single entity, they maintain their separate identities in what they now refer to as a "Social Memory Complex."

RA explained in the channeling sessions that they visited ancient Egypt thousands of years ago to dictate their message, which they call the "Law of One," as well as to teach the Egyptians how to build the pyramids, physical healing techniques, as well as to impart other information. But they stopped communicating with the Egyptians after a few hundred years because RA's message had been severely distorted. Since they did not accomplish their objective at that time, they felt obligated to return to Earth to dictate the Law of One again—this time to a group they believed had a lower probability of distorting their message.

At RA's level of evolution—the Sixth Density—ESP is used by entities to communicate with one another rather than spoken language or words, and of course, English was never used or spoken on Venus. Because of this, the language of the channeled material is unique and stilted, which often makes it difficult to understand. This is one reason I didn't take it seriously when I read it the first time. For example, instead of saying "person," "human," or "individual," RA will say "mind/body/spirit complex." RA uses words that they consider to be as accurate as possible, and to RA a person is a combination of mind, body, and spirit. However, because we are not familiar with the way words that RA chooses are used, what RA says often isn't clear, and the meaning is obscured. In my case, I have to stop and think and translate what RA has said into common, everyday English. After a while, of course, a reader will begin to get used to RA's form of speech.

You may want to read the RA books or listen to them yourself because they contain much, much more information than I will cover here. You can buy them in several forms such as Kindle, paperback and in audio on Amazon, or you can go to the website www.lawofone.info and actually read or listen to all 106 channeled sessions from the 1980s at no cost, whatsoever. There is also an excellent introduction to the RA material on YouTube by Aaron Abke, who appears to be a very impressive guy. I've watched a number of his videos and have come to consider him to be a sort of modern-day guru. When you get a chance, I suggest you put his name in the YouTube search space and "law of one," and be sure to start with Episode One.

With that being said, let me summarize as briefly as possible what RA has to say that will lay the groundwork for information that can raise your vibrational frequency and change your life for the better. According to RA, the purpose of the creation of the universe parallels Thomas Campbell's theory that expansion of consciousness is the goal, and this meant that the Source or the Creator had to find a way to come to know and experience him/her/itself. For this goal to be fully achieved required the evolution of consciousness in beings that are offshoots but remain part of the Creator. (From this point forward, I'm going to use the masculine pronoun for the Creator. Even though the Creator is not a "he" or a "she," I don't feel comfortable using the word "it.")

Since the Creator is all that is, he cannot step outside himself and know himself except by sending out pieces of himself that become seemingly separate, but in fact remain connected to and extensions of him. The Source is Infinite Consciousness and each one of us and all living things are sparks or pieces or bits of this Infinite Consciousness in the process of evolving toward reunification with him. The upshot is that your consciousness began as what might be thought of as one of these sparks, and it has evolved on

Earth, and perhaps other planets, from the very low level of consciousness that exists in matter, to the much higher level it is today, which happens to be the stage of awareness of self that RA refers to as Third Density. The Creator has experienced himself through you from your beginning, and he continues to experience himself through you as well as through everyone and everything in his creation.

The Creator has instilled in you and in all life the desire to evolve, and by pursuing this instinctive desire, you will eventually reunite with him. That's correct. No matter what, you will reunite with him someday, but there is still a long, long way to go. The vast majority of people alive on this planet remain in Third Density, and a minority has taken baby steps into Fourth Density. Over the course of evolution from the very beginning to reunification with the Creator, there are seven densities of consciousness, which means that once someone moves into the Fourth, he or she will still have Densities Five, Six, and Seven to go.

You may be aware that the number seven is an important number in metaphysics. No doubt you have heard of Seventh Heaven as the highest realm of heaven, and that is apparently true. The seven densities of consciousness correspond to each of the seven energy centers in the human body, or chakras, as well as to the seven musical notes on a scale, and the seven colors in the rainbow.

RA calls the seven densities "octaves" and explains that the evolution of consciousness within each octave works in seven major stages, or densities. A density has to do with the entanglement of light within a certain range of vibration. The lower the density, the slower the vibratory rate, and the slower the vibratory rate, the lower the capacity for the expression of consciousness. The higher densities have ever faster vibratory rates, thereby increasing the ability to express consciousness.

What drives evolution is the innate desire to increase our vibratory rate, and therefore, as we evolve, to achieve ever higher levels of consciousness, ultimately to reunite with the Creator. Yet all the while, we retain our awareness of self, and that will continue to be so when we eventually do achieve reunification. When that happens, what then will be our "Social Memory Complex" will become a new universe ready to begin the process all over again.

Brief Descriptions of the First Few Densities

The First Density is the initial state of being, which includes the four elements of earth, water, fire, and air. As the sun condensed into a star and the planets formed, the Earth spent quite a while in First Density. After about three-quarters of a billion years of rock, magma, water, and air interacting with one another, Second Density consciousness, characterized by growth and movement, evolved. Second Density includes all biological life and organic matter that has autonomous movement all the way from microbial life up to plants and animals.

Today's scientists tell us the universe began with a Big Bang 13.8 billion years ago, and that the earth formed about 4.5 billion years ago. They also say life began on Earth 3.77 billion years ago. So if current science is correct, that means 730 million years were required to move from First Density into Second Density. At that stage, consciousness became aware of different portions of itself communicating with other portions.

Among animals in the most advanced stage of Second Density evolution are those that have become pets, and through their interactions with humans, have been given a name, boundaries, and affection. Because of this, an animal begins to develop a sense of self-awareness, which means consciousness has begun evolving into Third Density.

Full Third Density is characterized by self-awareness and is the stage at which well over half of the people on Earth find themselves at present. Fortunately, it is the shortest stage in terms of incarnation cycles because it is also the most intense of all the seven densities. I say "fortunately" because it is the stage in which we suffer and encounter the most difficulty. According to RA, Third Density is at least one hundred times more difficult to navigate than any other level.

Two additional factors are hallmarks of Third Density: 1) the introduction of polarity and 2) what RA calls "the veil of forgetting." Although it is sometimes short-circuited, the veiling process shrouds our memories from previous incarnations so that we have no conscious awareness that we are on an evolutionary journey. This allows each of us to make an authentic choice between the positive and the negative polarities.

The catalyst spurring on evolution in Third Density is psychological suffering, and this is what makes the Third

Density extremely difficult in comparison to all the others. Our suffering forces us to seek freedom from the ego, which was built beginning at the very end of the Second Density and fostered well into our Third Density incarnations. Developing an ego was necessary because it is what allows each of us to eventually become autonomous and to truly possess free will. It seems to me this is what the allegory of Adam and Eve is about. By eating the fruit of the tree of the knowledge of good and evil, Adam and Eve became Third Density beings. Before that, they were nondual, Second Density beings such as animal wildlife from chipmunks to antelopes with no such knowledge and without free will.

The Source wants us to have free will because he experiences himself through us, and free will allows us to choose to do all sorts of things, which in turn allows him to experience a wide variety of adventures. Moreover, I suspect he wants us to eventually choose to be with and experience him without having been coerced, just as you would want your future spouse to have the freedom to choose you over others because you are the one he or she wants to be with.

Suffering, which RA calls "the catalyst" of evolution in the Third Density, is extremely high because we learn and evolve by facing and dealing with difficulties. Without hardship, there is little incentive to advance and overcome a situation. Without suffering and sorrow, we cannot truly develop compassion for others.

It also goes without saying that as Third Density beings, the egos we develop, which create the illusion we are separate from everyone and everything, cause us to become barbaric and hostile toward others, particularly during our initial incarnations as Third Density beings. This has been apparent throughout human history, and we can see it going on now, as I write this, in Russia's war on Ukraine.

Eventually, however, many Third Density souls learn the lessons of love and understanding and begin to remember that they are actually eternal beings having a temporary physical experience. When this realization has been reached, a choice must be made between the two polarities—positive or negative. If an entity decides he or she prefers the negative polarity, the person begins an evolutionary journey on what RA calls the "Service-to-Self" path. If he or she chooses the positive polarity, that human being begins a journey on the "Service-to-Others" path. RA doesn't see one path as good and the other as bad. As in Thomas Campbell's Big TOE, the Creator, Source, or Infinite Mind is simply exploring all the possibilities. I'm reminded of what Shakespeare's Hamlet said, "There is nothing either good or bad, but thinking makes it so." Nevertheless, RA says the Service-to-Self folks cannot and will not make it all the way back to the Source. They will have to switch polarities when they arrive in the Sixth Density, and that will not be easy.

It's important to know that everything about a soul's evolutionary journey forward hinges on this choice. If you have not already made the choice, the time has come. The Service-to-Others path follows Jesus' admonition to "love your neighbor as yourself," and in doing so, an entity uses his or her talents to serve others and thereby make the world a better place. Moreover, as you now know, it is one of the three keys to lasting happiness.

Things Go in Cycles

According to RA, Third Density on Earth, which is slowly and tumultuously coming to an end, consisted of three 25,000-year cycles, and we have recently gone past the end of the third cycle. We can actually see the shift to Fourth Density occurring because of the dramatic changes in social justice, equal rights for minorities, and awareness of global corruption, which have exploded recently. What has caused this is that the combined frequency of those alive today on the Service-to-Others route has reached 51 percent overall. This doesn't mean that 51 percent of the population of the earth is already on the Fourth Density path. Some people on it are further along than others, and therefore have higher frequencies than those with only a foothold. As a result, these more advanced souls contribute more than their fair share to the total combined frequency level. What is important to know is that our planetary frequency has become elevated to a point that makes a Fourth Density world possible.

The aforementioned shift began in 2012, and according to RA, everyone alive today will either become a Fourth Density being or remain in Third Density and repeat a Third Density 25,000 year cycle on another planet the next time they incarnate. This should give everyone a huge incentive to work on him or herself in order to make the shift.

Which Way Will Earth Go?

RA also said Fourth Density Service-to-Self and Service-to-Others human beings alive today will not inhabit the same planet during their next incarnations, nor will the billions who remain Third Density beings. Third Density folk will begin another evolutionary cycle somewhere else. Fourth Density Service-to-Others folks will be on a planet exploring, learning and enhancing the positive polarity in a society that I'm guessing will look like what Jesus referred to as "The Kingdom of Heaven." Those on the negative Fourth Density path will incarnate on a planet with a chaotic, negative Fourth Density reality, which seems to me a pretty hellish place to be, but apparently, it's where they will feel comfortable and belong.

The question I wonder about is which way planet Earth will go. Will it be a positive Fourth Density world or a negative Fourth Density world? I think that's the battle that's now underway, and I hope you will join me in doing what you can to make it positive. Service-to-Self individuals thrive on self-interest and subjugation of others. If they take over, Earth will not be a place I'd want to be. I've been to China, which is how I picture a negative Fourth Density world, and I wouldn't want to live there. The way to avoid it happening, I believe, is for as many people as possible to rebuff politicians and others who would divide us through diversity politics or who espouse outdated social dogma that some members of society are victims. What needs to happen is for everyone to understand that race is only skin deep and we are all one big family of humanity who should work together to support and encourage one another. Please do your part to get that message out.

Either way, whether the Earth goes in the Service-to-Self or in the Service-to-Others direction, in the long run I suppose it won't really matter. If Earth goes in the negative direction, people alive on Earth today who take the positive route will incarnate the next time around on a positive polarity Fourth Density planet somewhere else in the universe. Moreover, if enough people understand and take to heart the most important and biggest step in becoming a Four Density being, I believe Fourth Density will turn out positive for Earth as well. As I hope has been driven home, that step is to understand that there is only One Life of which we all are part, that each of us is the non-dual transcendent—Infinite Mind—at the core. We are truly brothers and sisters—all with the same "Father," and we need to take that seriously and behave toward one another in ways that demonstrate that.

As I hope this chapter has revealed, using your special talents and abilities in service to others is one of the three keys to lasting happiness. The question, then, is what your special talents are, and how can they best be put to work? That's what we are going to explore in the next chapter.

Chapter Four
Know Thyself

Below I have laid out a series of questions, the answers to which will give you valuable insight about yourself, including who you are and what line of work or activity best suits you that will also bring the highest sense of fulfillment.

Each person is unique. We all want different things. Different things motivate us. We have different purposes, aims, values, needs, drives, impulses and urges. And this is good. Imagine how boring life would be if everyone wanted the same things and thought the same way.

Although no one is exactly like you, there are others who are similar. According to a widely used system of categorizing character and temperament types, 16 basic types exist. Determining which you fall into and the general characteristics of your type will help you better understand yourself. This will prepare you for a timeout I'm going to suggest you take to determine your mission and purpose, and therefore what you ought to be doing with your life.

The following questions are divided into four categories. Circle the letter for the answer that best fits your thinking and preferences. Be honest. There are no right or wrong answers. Which one best describes you?

These questions will determine whether you give yourself an I or an E (circle one or the other for each):

E — I like to go to social events and interact with lots of people, or
I — I would prefer to stay home and read a book or watch television.

E — I like to know a little about a lot of things, or
I — I prefer to know a lot about a few things that really interest me.

E — I usually hate to leave a party, my energy seems to increase as time passes, or
I — I usually prefer to leave a party when I run out of steam.

E — I like to keep up with what's going on with my friends, or
I — I often get behind on what's going on with friends.

E — People say I'm very approachable, or
I — Sometimes people think I'm somewhat reserved and they hesitate to approach me.

E — When the phone rings, I am usually the first to get it, or
I — When the phone rings, I usually let someone else answer it.

Did you have more Es or Is? _____
(We'll discuss later what to do if it's a tie)

The Three Keys

The next group of questions will determine whether you give yourself an S or an N. Again, there are no right or wrong answers. Be honest.

S — I prefer to base my decisions firmly on experience, or
N — I think hunches often pay off so I pay close attention to them when making a decision.

S — I prefer to associate with sensible, down to earth people, or
N — I like to be around really imaginative people.

S — I'm more interested in what actually exists, or
N — I'm usually more interested in what can be.

S — When I do something, I normally do it the time-honored, usual way, or
N — I often have my own way of doing things that works for me.

S — I believe that facts are simply that—the way things are, or
N — I believe that facts illustrate principles.

S — I find so-called visionaries somewhat annoying, or
N — I find visionaries rather fascinating.

Did you have more Ss or Ns? _____
(We'll discuss later what to do if it's a tie)

The Three Keys

The next group of questions will determine whether you give yourself a T or an F. Again, there are no right or wrong answers. Be honest.

T — I'm more impressed by principles, or
F — I'm more impressed by emotions.

T — I would rather people think of me as a logical person, or
F — I would rather people think of me as a sentimental person.

T — I'm more often a cool-headed person, or
F — I'd say I'm more often a warmhearted person.

T — When I make decisions, I feel more comfortable basing them on standards, or
F — I feel more comfortable basing them on feelings.

T — In judging others, I'm more likely to be swayed by principles, or
F — I'm more likely to be swayed by circumstances.

T — I'd say my head usually rules, or
F — I'd say my heart usually rules.

Did you have more Ts or Fs? _____
(We'll discuss later what to do if it's a tie)

The Three Keys

The final group of questions will determine whether you give yourself a J or a P. Again, there are no right or wrong answers. Be honest.

J — I prefer to work toward a deadline, or
P — I prefer to work without a deadline.

J — I usually choose rather carefully, or
P — I often choose rather impulsively.

J — I prefer to be on time, or
P — I'm often rather casual about time.

J — I feel more comfortable once things are settled, or
P — I feel more comfortable when things are open-ended.

J — I like to have things planned out, or
P — I prefer to let things happen.

J — I'd say I'm more deliberate than spontaneous, or
P — I'd say I'm more spontaneous than deliberate.

Did you have more Js or Ps? _____
Now write out the letters of your personality type. For example, my personality type is INTJ. Yours is _____.

You have just taken a quiz that should indicate your personality type based on the Myers-Briggs scale. If you

The Three Keys

had a tie between two letters, go back and take another look at the questions. If you have difficulty deciding which letter best describes you, you are likely a combination of two personality types. This is not unusual. Read about both. Decide which is the closest or best description of you. You may be a combination of the two.

There are eight components to the M-B personality types:

E = Extroverts: Skilled with multitasking and fast-paced work environments. Extroverts gather their energy while in groups of people.
I = Introverts: Works well in smaller groups or alone, and prefers to take on tasks one at a time.
N = Intuitives: Skilled with identifying patterns and thinking creatively to solve problems. Thinks broadly and sees the big picture.
S = Sensors: Detail oriented and focuses on facts and data. Applies common sense and past experiences to problem solving.
T = Thinkers: Prefers to think logically, while maintaining consistency across all processes.
F = Feelers: Cooperative and often sensitive, they make decisions based on the feelings of others.
J = Judgers: Values order and preparation, prefers to stick to the rules and always works with a plan.
P = Perceivers: A little on the spontaneous side, they prefer to have many options and are flexible when carrying out tasks.

The Three Keys

Using these components, the Myers-Briggs system then assigns one of sixteen personality types to the individual taking its test. Overall, the system provides greater depth when compared to the more simplistic extrovert or introvert approach. For example, your outcome could be "INTP," which is composed of Introvert, iNtuitive, Thinker, and Perceiver. You read that right—intuitive is marked as "N" in order to avoid confusion. To learn all about your personality type, later you can go online to Google and search your four letters. You will find that there is a lot of information about your personality type. To get you started now, here is a brief overview of the careers and job types that would best suit each of the sixteen types:

ESFJ: This personality type tends to prefer working in groups, especially in roles where they care for the well-being of others. Good careers for those with the ESFJ personality type are social worker, nurse or healthcare worker, sales representative, or in public relations.

ESTJ: This group often seeks leadership roles or roles that otherwise require them to make important decisions. Suitable career paths include lawyer, project manager, pharmacist, or insurance agent.

ESFP: Those who fall under the ESFP group tend to prefer roles in which they can interact with others on a regular basis. Some good career choices for the ESFP group include primary care physician, interior designer, actor, or child welfare counselor.

ENTP: This group likes taking chances and enjoys a good challenge. Those who received an ENTP on their test prefer to not conform to certain norms and can be persistent in their goals. They would be a great fit in roles such as marketing director, politician, creative director, or as an entrepreneur.

ESTP: This personality type craves excitement and shows their true potential while under stress. They prefer high-stakes roles in which they can be resourceful, such as detective, investor, sports coach, or entertainment agent.

ENTJ: These individuals prefer to have a well thought out strategy, and think logically and analytically. Roles in which they can create order and maximize efficiency are their favorite types, and their best career choices could be as a lawyer, a market research analyst, an executive, or a venture capitalist.

ENFP: This group is creative and likes to keep an open mind. They prefer roles in which they can be expressive while communicating with others, such as journalist, creative director, event planner, or consultant.

ENFJ: Those who fall under this category are social butterflies, tend to be very energetic, and prefer roles in which they work cooperatively with others. Some potential career paths for those who received ENFJ are sales manager, HR specialist, advertising executive, or in public relations.

The Three Keys

INTP: This personality type prefers to work independently, and solves problems that require precision, as well as some creativity. Good career paths include programmer, software engineer, architect, or college professor.

ISTP: This individual prefers to take on roles in which they master the tools of their trade. Those with the ISTP personality type tend to prefer taking action, and good career paths for them are pilot, emergency room physician, data communications analyst, or civil engineer.

ISTJ: This group is dedicated to their responsibilities and works best in roles that highlight their ability to be reliable to others. Career options include accountant, government employee, auditor, or CFO (chief financial officer).

ISFJ: This personality type enjoys helping others, and prefers to work in roles in which they can provide a service, such as dentist, elementary school teacher, customer service representative, or librarian.

INTJ: Those who fall under the INTJ category are perfectionists, and prefer to work in roles where they don't have to interact with others quite as much. Some good career paths for this personality type are software developer, executive, consultant, architect, personal finance advisor, or investment banker.

ISFP: This group uses their sensitivity and strong empathetic nature to help others. Roles in which they can show their strengths best are physical therapist, massage therapist, fashion designer, or landscape architect.

INFP: This individual is a deep thinker. They like to use their compassion and adaptability in roles such as graphic designer, psychologist, writer, or physical therapist.

INFJ: Those who received the INFJ type on the Myers-Briggs test are typically creative people who are motivated by their values and integrity. Good career choices for this personality type are social worker, customer service manager, or school counselor.

Keep in mind that like all personality tests, the Myers-Briggs test isn't 100% accurate, but combined with the exercises in the upcoming chapter, I believe it will be helpful in determining how to put your abilities and talents to work in service to others. At some point, perhaps right after you finish reading this book, I suggest you go to Google and enter your letters in the search engine—nothing more or less, just the letters. A number of sites will come up where you can read all about your personality and temperament profile. You will also likely come across careers and job categories that may appeal to you in addition to those listed above.

Chapter Five
Take a Timeout to
Determine Your Mission

We are eternal spiritual beings who incarnate on earth for specific reasons. In addition to learning specific lessons or settling karma, we likely have something we are here to do. We're like snowflakes in that each human being is unique and has certain talents and abilities that he or she can put to use to help others in ways no one else can quite as well. Discovering what that is and determining the best way to use those abilities will point you to a path that will take you to lasting happiness. That's what this chapter is meant to do.

Take a Full Day to Pinpoint Your Path

As soon as possible once you have finished reading this book, set aside a full day. It might be a Saturday or a Sunday, or some other day you have off from work or school. Plan to spend six to eight consecutive hours alone, except for bathroom breaks and lunch. Go to a library or some secluded place. Leave your cell phone and computer in the car because you don't want to be disturbed. Take a pen or half a dozen pencils and a legal pad, find a quiet spot, and get comfortable. You are there to decide what to do with the rest of your life. Nothing you can do is more important.

Here are some sample questions you might ask and answer to get you warmed up. Spend some serious time with each one you decide to tackle:

- Who am I?
- Where am I going?
- What is my purpose in life?
- If I had one month to live, what regrets would I have?
- Am I happy, and if not, why not?
- Am I healthy? If not, why not?
- Am I getting out of life all that life has to offer?
- Do I love my job and love getting up on Monday mornings? If not, why not? What can I do about it?
- What are my goals, desires and passions in life?
- If money were no issue, what would I really want to do with my life?
- What am I doing right and what am I doing wrong?
- What do I need to do more of, or less of to get the most out of life?
- Am I the best parent, the best spouse, the best student, the best person that I can be? If not, what needs to change?

An approach a friend of mine took that led to big, positive changes and a better life was to write at the top of the first page of his legal pad, "I am now 101 years old, I am on my deathbed, and I'm looking back. If I'd stayed on the course I was on when I was at (the age you are now), would I have any regrets? Instead, having identified the paths I was on and made the proper course corrections, I have lived an incredibly successful and fulfilling life. What about it was most important to me? What were my biggest accomplishments? What else stands out?"

Whichever way you decide to go when it comes to questions, write down everything, and I mean everything that comes to mind. As you do this, it is important to be totally objective. Do not approach any of the questions with preconceived ideas about what the answers might be. Instead, pretend you are a friend or an advisor who knows you well but is totally objective and not emotionally involved in any thing, one way or the other. And do not self-edit; take your time. Taking time and having time to take is important because your mind works differently when you feel rushed because of a looming deadline. It's virtually impossible to go deep with a clock ticking in your head. This is also something you cannot do riding in a car to and from work or the grocery store. It's important for you to be totally relaxed and in position to be laser-focused. That's why you need to set aside an entire day.

Okay, let's say you're in that library cubicle. No phones. No computers. Sit back and let go. Take a deep breath and hold it to the count of four. Then let it out slowly through your mouth. There's nothing else to do or to think about but the life ahead of you and what you want it to become. Ask a question and start writing what pops into your head.

Once you reach a point where you cannot think of anything else, go back, look over what you have written and arrange the items in descending order with the most important one first.

The Three Keys

Having completed that task, go to the next blank sheet and put the number-one most important thing at the top. Then write down what is keeping you from achieving that goal or taking care of that issue. Is it something buried in your unconscious mind? Did someone in your family or a teacher tell you what you wanted out of life was impossible and you believed it? Pull all that negative stuff out, put it on paper, and see it in the light of day for what it really is: hogwash. Later, when you leave the library, take with you the sheets of paper with hogwash written on them and burn them as soon as you get a chance. Consider that all that negative stuff has gone up in smoke. It's behind you now and no longer impedes you in any way.

Obstacles Point to Your Path

Okay, once you have eliminated unconscious programming and hogwash issues, what is left standing in your way? Obstacles are what you want to find as you go through this exercise. Once you identify them, half the work is done because now all you need to do is figure out ways to get around them, over them, or under them.

Read this and let it sink in:

The course you devise to skirt the obstacles standing between you and your goals will be your action plan. That is the path to take to get where you want to be.

Let's say you want to be a substance abuse counselor and the obstacle is that you don't have the right degree. You need to figure out a way to get that degree—that's your path. A friend that had spent a number of years as a radio disc jockey was able to do just that and is now a substance abuse counselor in a state prison system. I saw him the other day, and he had a big smile on his face. He loves what he does and feels fulfilled because he has found his purpose and is pursuing it.

Perhaps, you say, that makes sense, but I don't have the money.

You have just identified the obstacle: money.

A friend of mine, a mechanical engineer who worked at General Motors designing cars, decided in his thirties he wanted to be a doctor. He realized that was his calling. So he sold his house so he could use the equity from it, and he also took out college loans. It was a long grind and wasn't easy, but he is now a doctor and happy as can be.

Another friend, a successful insurance salesman, did the same thing, and he had a wife and two small children in tow. He sold his house so he could go to seminary and now is a very successful Christian minister.

Okay, you say, but you haven't told me how to find what I should be doing that will really and truly turn me on, and after doing what you just recommended, I still haven't figured it out. What should I do now?

As stated above, we each have a unique combination of talents and abilities that enable us to serve others in ways no one else is quite able to do. It's something you are especially good at, something you can do better than anyone else. It's called your Dharma. Somewhere deep down, what I call your Higher Self and those of a religious bent

The Three Keys

call the soul, that part of you knows exactly what it is. It is the reason you came to earth this time around. Putting your Dharma to work in service to others is your purpose. That's your path to fulfillment, success in life, and dare I say, bliss. You can begin determining what it is by answering these questions:

- When growing up, what did people tell you that you were gifted at or had a talent for, i.e., what were you always being recognized, admired, scolded or reprimanded for?
- What did you do well growing up that seemed unusual or unique?
- What do you really like to do?
- What activity causes you to lose all sense of time?
- What are you doing when you find yourself in a groove?
- What do you do that taps into some innate ability?
- What are you drawn to doing?
- What things do you pick up or learn to do much faster than others? List them.
- What are you sensitive to and notice that others usually don't?
- What activity would you do if money were not an issue?
- What can you do that you can't explain how you do it when asked about it?

The Three Keys

All the questions above ultimately lead to this one, which I think of has the Big Kahuna:

What have I done that puts me so totally in the zone that when I finish, I look up and see that hours have passed and it seemed like only minutes?

That activity points to your Dharma. Once you put your finger on it, what you need to do is determine how to use that activity to be of service to others. Then make that your life's work, and you will be on your way to a truly satisfying and fulfilling life.

In my case, it was making movies. That's right, at about eleven or twelve years old, I got an eight millimeter movie camera for Christmas, and I started making films. I loved putting images together in sequences that told a story and communicated a message. I spent hours on end doing so and when I was engaged in that activity the time flew by—because I was "in the flow."

In college, I put the same desire and energy to work. I drew cartoons for the newspaper, worked on the yearbook, and became Editor-in-Chief my senior year—a paid position. When I graduated, I went into advertising and continued creating communications. But after fifteen years or so of using my talents and abilities to sell other businesses' products, it began to get old. Something was missing—I felt like "I'd been there and done that." So I started getting up an hour early each morning and using that time to write what I wanted to write, which delivered a message I thought would benefit others. Within a year, I'd written a book, and lo and behold it got published. I kept doing that, and today I'm a full time author with more than three dozen books in print. Now, that's how I use my talents and abilities in service to others, and I love what I do. As a result, time not only continues to fly by when I'm at it, I've achieved what you can also achieve—lasting happiness—if you follow the path set out for you by this book.

About Your Dharma

Allow me to explain the concept of Dharma. According to a professor at the College of Metaphysics in Missouri, Dharma is a Sanskrit word meaning "statute" or "law." She once told me Dharma is the law that orders the universe and the essential nature or function of a person or a thing. It is what we each have to give or to share with others. Even though a person may be good at something, he or she isn't fulfilling her Dharma if that person is primarily after acclaim or money. People who are using their Dharma in the most productive ways tend to be humble, which is not to say they don't or won't receive acclaim. Many do, but they are likely to feel the acclaim is not really deserved because they so thoroughly enjoy what they do and it comes so naturally to them.

"It is your soul's urge," the metaphysics professor said. "When you are responding to your Dharma, you feel at peace. Someday, after you grow old and look back at life, you will regard the time you spent putting your Dharma to work as the golden years. This is because people who are using their Dharma are passionate about what they do, as though it were a flame burning in them. They lose track of time. They're in the flow. And something else: Each person applies his or her Dharma in a way that is unique as though each of us is one piece of a giant jigsaw puzzle and we fit together to make up a whole."

There you have it. Identify your Dharma and develop a plan to get off the wrong career path and onto the path to your bliss, which is putting your Dharma to work in the service of others. That's the Universe's intention for you, why you came to Earth, and how you can make a living by doing what you enjoy.

Perhaps you are thinking that all sounds well and good, but I probably will not be able to make a whole lot of money doing what I love. I will not argue about that. Maybe it's true. The question is whether you can make enough to put a roof over your head and food on the table, which brings to mind an observation made recently by the pastor of my church in one of his sermons. If you earn the minimum wage, which based on my state's rate today translates to about $24,000 per year, and you suddenly get a raise to $100,000, your life will change dramatically and your sense of happiness and contentment will very likely increase—at least for a while. But if you make $100,000 per year and get an increase to $500,000, your life probably will not be all that different. Certainly, you will feel a momentary sense of joy. You might decide to throw a party. But as time marches on, your life will not fundamentally change. Oh, you might trade in your Toyota Camry and buy a Maserati. You might sell your house on Elm Street and buy a bigger one on Grove. But the Camry was already getting you where you wanted to go, and the house on Elm kept out the rain and the cold and probably had central air.

The people I know who make half a million a year do not appear any happier than those who make considerably less. As previously stated, the cliché is true: "Money can't buy love," and it can't buy happiness. Lasting happiness is found within and by doing what you love, which means using your Dharma in service to others. So as long as you can make enough money to buy the basics, which include food, shelter, clothing, transportation, and medical care, why not go for it?

All right, then, let's say you have determined your Dharma and how you can put it to work in service to others. What will it take to get off the current, wrong path, and onto the path to your bliss? It will take time, and it will take a plan. So identify the obstacles and work out a step-by-step plan and timetable to get around them. Keep taking full-day timeouts as often as possible in order to put your plan down on paper, and don't stop taking timeouts once you have done so. I suggest you set aside a full day once each month to update, add to, and refine the plan.

And don't be naïve about this process. Understand and accept that it will take time and perseverance. Taking ten or fifteen minutes to meditate every day, and a full day each month to think and plan will be important. In between, listen to the still small voice within. Review your life and think about the decisions that brought you where you are today and where the new ones you have identified are taking you.

In your day-a-month library time, think back and try to remember why your Higher Self chose the circumstances of your birth. Why did you pick those particular parents? There had to be a reason. Was it something they could teach you? Did they seem like good, caring people who would let you follow your bliss? Were the circumstances right for creating situations that would enable you to put your Dharma into practice? I can tell you this: I've reached the age when I can look back on my life and see how such things were in place for me and why I selected the time, the place, and the parents I did. Now, it all makes perfect sense.

I suggest you take the time to do the same because it will help keep you motivated. After all, this is your life.

Don't you want to make the most of it?

Chapter Six
Go for It

Unless you suffer from a terminal illness and your doctors have said you don't have much longer to live, it's not too late to change directions and head toward a life of lasting happiness—no matter what your age. With that in mind, let's review and summarize the three keys:

1. The feeling and belief that you are an integral part of the whole

Plenty of evidence clearly indicates there's more to reality than matter. Intelligence must have come first for the DNA molecule to form and for complex organs like eyes, ears, the brain, kidneys, livers and so forth—not to mention the panda's thumb—to have developed. It seems obvious to me, and it ought to seem obvious to you, that consciousness is the ground of being and that we're all characters in what might be thought of as a dream the Infinite Mind or Source is having. You and I are chips off the block of Infinite Mind. We are all connected, and we are all integral parts of the whole. Like snowflakes, no two of us are exactly alike. That means you are a special person who can provide benefits to others in ways no one else can.

By the way, to supplement that knowledge and the feeling of companionship it gives, I suggest you also consider becoming a part of a like-minded group—perhaps a service club, a book or bridge club, or a sports club or team, or the congregation of a church, a Sunday school class, or spiritual study group.

2. Using your special talents and abilities in service to others

No two people are alike. We each have a unique set of talents and abilities. We can use them to pile up treasure on earth—treasure we cannot take with us—or we can use them to pile up treasure in heaven. We do the latter when we use our talents and abilities in service to others. It's interesting to note that according to thousands of near death survivors who have passed over and returned, after we die we will have a detailed life review during which we will see and *feel* how our words and our actions affected others from their points of view. That's right, we will actually experience the emotions they felt. It seems to me that's what Jesus was talking about when he told the rich young ruler to, "sell what you possess and give to the poor, and you will have treasure in heaven." (See Matthew 19:21)

Not only that, by making the choice to use our talents and abilities in service to others, we are reserving a place in Fourth Density, aka the Kingdom of Heaven on Earth, the next time we incarnate—maybe even this time around if Earth makes the transition soon enough. What could possibly be better than that?

3. The knowledge and belief that you are an eternal being

Nihilism is for Scientific Materialists who ignore the facts. In other words, Nihilism is pure BS. At the core you are a unique whirlpool of ground-of-being consciousness, a spark of the Divine or Infinite Mind—a one-of-a-kind formation of non-dual transcendent energy that cannot be destroyed, and you are evolving toward reunification with the Source. Even after reunification, you will maintain your unique identity and consciousness. The upshot is you will be around for eternity, so you might as well begin now to become someone you will enjoy being... forever.

You Now Know the Truth, Don't You Wish Everyone Did?

Scientific Materialism has served its purpose. It has brought us all kinds of advancements in technology and medicine, as well as labor saving devices and machinery. But it is time for science to be updated to include the unseen part of reality because without the knowledge that the unseen exists and that it supports and informs the material world, the unavoidable conclusion is that death is the end—and that can only lead to Nihilism.

Materialism encourages us to look out for number one at the expense of everyone else, to go for the gusto and "make something of ourselves," which means we should climb the corporate ladder or start a business selling snake oil in order to accumulate power and wealth. It almost never occurs to us to reach out and use our abilities to make the world a better place, and if it does occur to us, we are likely to start thinking we must be some kind of wimp.

Perhaps this should not be surprising. We live in the Information Age—with the result that so much comes at us every day it's almost impossible to stop and think. This may be one reason the water building up behind the dam that's holding back our understanding of the true nature of reality has not yet broken through. Maybe so much information has caused our minds to go numb and so we simply ignore the truth as little more than white noise—even when it stares us in the face.

Nevertheless, the time has come to acknowledge that we are all connected and the way to happiness and fulfillment is to recognize it and base our life's work on that fact. We are not comparable to machines—as the nineteenth-twentieth century paradigm still holding sway would have us believe. We are not assemblies of parts that somehow evolved out of the muck and developed a computer-like organ called the brain that miraculously creates awareness inside our skulls. When the brain dies, the lights do not go out. We simply leave the old worn out vehicle behind and move on to a different reality—the unseen reality.

The brain and the body are simply the means to an end. The brain-body combination is a way for spirit—the life force, a spark of the godhead, the Source or Infinite Mind—to enter into physical reality. You're here now, and it's likely you have been here hundreds if not thousands of times before. Why not make this time the best time—

maybe even the last time before you incarnate in Fourth Density?

Just think how greatly things would change for the better if everyone knew what you now know—that we are all eternal. That death is not the end. That death cannot provide an escape because death does not exist. That there is only life. That each of us is like the character in the movie, *Groundhog Day*. Just imagine how much better off the world will be when everyone realizes that. We each will be motivated to get things right, and when we finally do, we will create heaven on Earth—aka positive Fourth Density—and in so doing achieve lasting happiness and the end of suffering. You can do that right now. There is absolutely no reason for you to wait.

What and who is holding the rest of humanity back? Those with a vested interest in maintaining the status quo, which includes politicians who keep us divided by playing one group against another. It's also so-called scientists who do their best to perpetuate Scientific Materialism—perhaps because they have been teaching students erroneous information and do not want to look stupid by admitting the truth. Others holding things back include people with dogmatic and counterproductive religious beliefs. I'm thinking, for example, of those who believe in an unforgiving, wrathful and capricious God, which is the antithesis of what many, including myself, believe and have actually experienced firsthand.

I'll let you in on a secret: The only people who go to hell are those who believe that's where they belong.

The Three Keys

I hope everyone who reads this book will get the message and spread the word. There's a battle going on—between what RA calls Service-to-Others and Service-to-Self individuals as well as between those who know the truth and those who strive to keep everyone ignorant of it.

I'll close by saying that now you know what Jesus meant when he said, "The truth will set you free." (See John 8:31-32) You know because you've just been set free. You now know that all creation is one connected whole with no separate pieces. We are the whole, and the whole is us. So do your part. Use your talents. Pitch in. Achieve lasting happiness and enjoy eternal life.

I'll leave you with this final thought, which was inspired by Voltaire's famous satire, *Candide, ou l'Optimisme* (1759). Concentrate on cultivating and improving your small piece of the big garden we live in called Earth. Just imagine how wonderful the world would be if everyone simply did that.

# # #

If you enjoyed this book and felt it was worthwhile reading, please take a moment to let others know by going to Amazon and rating it. You don't have to write a review, but that would be nice, too.

About Stephen Hawley Martin

Stephen Hawley Martin is a former marketing executive and consultant and the author of more than three-dozen books, including five published novels, half a dozen business management titles, and quite a few self-help books and metaphysical investigations. He is a former principal of the world-renowned advertising agency, The Martin Agency, the firm that created the GEICO Gecko and "Virginia is for lovers." Today, Stephen is editor and publisher of The Oaklea Press. Listed in *Who's Who in America,* and best known as a award-winning author, Steve is the only three-time winner of the *Writer's Digest* Book Award, having won twice for fiction and once for nonfiction. He has also won First Prize for Visionary Fiction from *Independent Publisher* and First Prize for Nonfiction from *USA Book News.* He and his wife of 35 years live in central Virginia.

To get in touch with Stephen and learn about other books he has written, visit his website:

www.shmartin.com

This two-book volume contains the bestselling title, *Life After Death, Powerful Evidence You Will Never Die* and the sequel, *Heaven, Hell & You.* As one reviewer, a medical doctor, wrote: "Extraordinary findings . . . will keep readers on the edge of their seats as they burn through this well written book's pages."

Kindle: ASIN: B07J46QQW8
Paperback: ISBN-10: 1727782038

If you believe that soul growth is the overarching reason we incarnate on Earth, this book was written for you. In it Stephen Hawley Martin describes in detail an incredible, mystical experience he had, and he shares insights he brought back with him that explain how you can raise your vibration to the next level in order to achieve joy in this life and bliss in the next.

Kindle: ASIN: B09GHY3SRN
PB: ISBN 979-8479020360

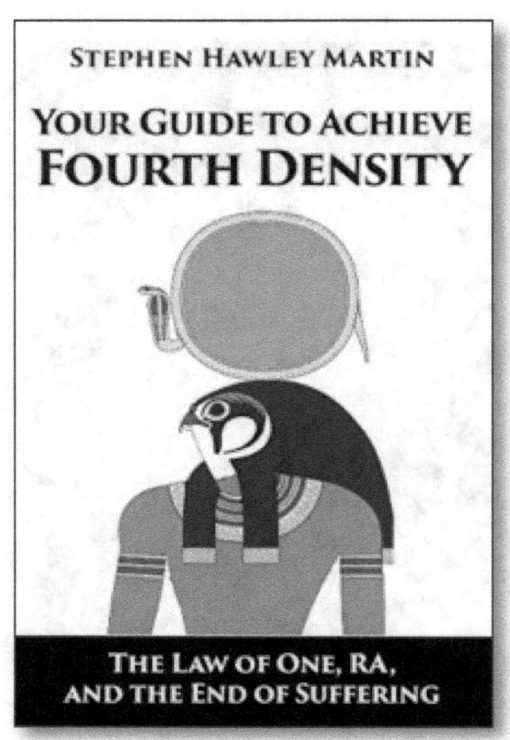

If you believe you are, or that you might be a spiritual being having a physical experience and wonder why you're here on Earth, this book provides the answers. Read it with an open mind. If you take to heart and follow the guidance it gives, your suffering might not vanish entirely, but you will be better able to deal with the little that remains.

Kindle: ASIN: B08CYBNZX4
PB: ISBN: 979-8666306222

You may believe humans are spiritual beings having a physical experience, but are you sure why we're here and what we ought to do about it? This book will tell this you this and much, much more because, as the record shows, the accuracy of information revealed by Edgar Cayce's more than 14,000 psychic readings was nothing less than extraordinary.

Kindle: ASIN: B07L7GF3HH
Paperback: ISBN-10: 1790978114

All the knowledge of the universe resides within you because at a deep level all minds, past and present, are connected. Everything that has ever happened, every thought, every idea is there. The trick is to draw out information when you need it. In this book Stephen explains how he learned to do so and how you can, too.

Kindle: ASIN: B07HHFFWP8
Paperback: ISBN-10: 1723835250

This 5-Star rated, fast-paced thriller is based on the true nature of reality as revealed in the book you hold in your hands. The heroine travels to the Caribbean Island of Martinque to save her father and learns the secret of life in the process. A page-turner, this novel won First Place for Fiction from *Writer's Digest* and First Place for Visionary Fiction from *Independent Publisher* magazine.

Kindle: ASIN: B08S7MG4WM
Paperback: ASIN: B08SB6VG9L

www.ingramcontent.com/pod-product-compliance
Lightning Source LLC
Chambersburg PA
CBHW072104110526
44590CB00018B/3305